This workbook belongs to:

_____

The Addiction Recovery Workbook

Dear Reader,

Thanks for purchasing my book.

I feel grateful to serve you with,
The Addiction Recovery Workbook

And I sincerely hope you enjoy, learn
and find what you're looking for.

All the best,

CW. V. Straaten

Would you like the first chapter of an audiobook version of this book?
Send an email to cw.vanstraaten@yahoo.com

Title the email "Recovery"

And I will send you the exercises for Free.

Copyright © 2018 C.W. V. Straaten

Published By: The Alexander Publishing House

ISBN: 9781983721731

All rights reserved.

No part of this publication may be reproduced, distributed, or transmitted in any form or by any means, including photocopying, recording, or other electronic or mechanical methods, without the prior written permission of the publisher, except in the case of brief quotations embodied in critical reviews and certain other noncommercial uses permitted by copyright law. For permission requests, write to the publisher.

Disclaimer

This book is not intended to act as a substitute for medical advice or treatment. Any person with a condition requiring medical attention should consult a qualified medical practitioner or suitable therapist.

The information provided in this book is stated to be truthful and consistent, in that any liability, in terms of inattention or otherwise, by any usage or abuse of any policies, processes, or directions contained within is the solitary and utter responsibility of the recipient reader. Under no circumstances will any legal responsibility or blame be held against the publisher for any reparation, damages, or monetary loss due to the information herein, either directly or indirectly.

The Addiction Recovery Workbook

A 7-Step Masterplan
To Take Back Control Of Your Life

Written By A Former Addict
BY C.W. V. STRAATEN

Instagram: become_recovery

True Potential Project 2018

Table of Contents

A Message From The Author

The Claws of Addiction

How To Read This Workbook

Note To The Reader

Step 1 - Quitting The Pattern

Step 2 - Replace Your Addiction & Find Peace

Relapse, encouragement

Step 3 - Take Responsibility & Educate Yourself On Addiction

Step 4 - Create 1 New Habit

Step 5 - Meet Your Addiction & Rewrite The Script

Relapse, What To Do When You Relapse

Step 6 - Create A New Vision & Start Today

Step 7 - Stay Inspired

The Nature Of Addiction, A Final Chapter

The End

Inspiration & Education

A 90-Day Recovery Journal

*A man who can't bear to share his habits
is a man who needs to quit them.*

Stephen King, *The Dark Tower*

A Message From The Author

First of all, I am deeply grateful
that you've purchased this workbook.

I've written this workbook first and foremost for you, the struggling addict. I wrote it because I know from experience that it can destroy your life. I wrote it because I can't stand to see so many wonderful souls being torn down by the devilish claws of addiction.

I wrote it because I know there can be a way out. Even for the worst struggling addict.

Daily Recovery Inspirations

If you want Daily Recovery Inspirations follow me on Instagram. I have created this page to help you focus on becoming free from addiction & focus on recovery every day.

Instagram: become_recovery

Or you can search on C.W. V. Straaten

The Claws of Addiction

"That you may live every day of your life."

Jonathan Swift

On the surface, there was nothing wrong with me. I was renting my own apartment, had a decent job, and a kind face for almost everyone. Each day I went to work, where I behaved like a decent employee. Every weekend I went out with friends and, on more than one occasion, had a few too many drinks. But everyone does, right? I was nice to my family, nice to my neighbors, nice to unknown people in the street. But when I returned to my apartment and locked the door and closed the curtains, I was confronted with my secrets. The debts that kept piling up, loneliness, boredom, and the one solution that numbed all of my problems.

During the Christmas holidays, I had a week off. It was supposed to be a fun time. Days where you don't have to do anything. Socializing with friends, seeing your grandparents for a change, cleaning your room, and reading that one book that you've looked forward to for months. All the while the atmosphere in the streets is one of kindness and warmth. Christmas is coming and everyone seems a bit more friendly. Peaceful, but I couldn't see it since the curtains of my apartment were closed.

I was constantly checking my bank account, waiting for the extra salary I was getting in December. It was the 24th of December and I was laying in my bed in my messy apartment with three empty beer cans on my desk, with a pair of trousers and my new, expensive shirt on the ground. I was looking at my phone. 3:11 PM. The money would be there at any moment. And I needed it. Oh, I desperately needed it. No more than one hour ago did I lose over 300 Euros betting on Dutch soccer. I didn't have a single dime left, not even to buy some Christmas presents. When my salary came in, all of these problems would be solved and I could finally sing along to Paul McCartney's Wonderful Christmastime.

One hour later. Most stores were almost closed. I had to hurry, but I was watching a live soccer match. One more goal and I would win almost 500 Euros. I was still in my bed. The curtains were still closed. It could have been the first of February, the middle of October. Does time matter in the hour of desperation? In the distance, I heard an ambulance and the notes of a well known Christmas melody. I needed one goal. It would solve my financial situation. It would solve my depression. It would solve everything.

Three minutes were left to play. I thought about my family, I thought about the calmness, the serene, joyful feeling that of these wonderful days. And boy, did I want to be a part of it. Time was ticking indifferently. It's unbelievable to believe that you could lose an entire paycheck within one hour. You could lose everything you hold dear, for that matter, within one hour. Addiction has the enormous power to destroy conscientiousness and sensibility. It is a storm that could destroy what one has built up for months within mere minutes.

A shout, a curse. A slap against the wall. It's time. No goal. No money. No solution anymore. I watch my laptop screen in agony. The screen turns black: the live stream is over. I check my account balance, just to be certain. There it is, an indifferent, cold zero.

Your Lowest Point In Life

We addicts, or people with seriously detrimental bad habits, all know of situations like this. Maybe not as dramatic, or maybe way more dramatic. We know the stories of the husband that steals his children's college money to feed his gambling habits, or a mother that continues to drug herself while raising her children, or the boss who sexually intimidates his employees. Tough stories that speak to the imagination. It's what we link addiction to. Alcohol, drugs, gambling, sex.

But what about the millions of people who suffer from bad habits in the confidence and security of their own homes?

Housewives playing Facebook games for hours a day, the young professional who binge-watches Netflix every night, the young student who spends entire days checking social media. And so on. These habits might seem a bit more trivial, but they all have the same effect: you don't see the real problem anymore.

Every bad habit and every addiction serves a purpose. It grants you instantaneous pleasure. You can attain it without much effort. It won't take any effort to grab a fourth beer on Tuesday night, eat your third piece of apple pie in the middle of the night, or play that video game. (Only in the last stages of a destroying addiction does it become difficult to continue the habit, due to either a lack of money, the possibility that others might find out, or because you've made it difficult for yourself to continue. For example, not being in control of your own money anymore).

"People are not meant to be on this earth just to fight an addiction."

Back to my gambling story. Unfortunately, that wasn't the last time I gambled, but it was one of my last episodes. I've lost tens of thousands of Euros over my seven years of gambling. I lost an insane number of hours aimlessly watching live sporting streams in the middle of the night, tired and irritated while losing over and over again. There were points where continuing to smile seemed to be an option no more. Times where I couldn't see the near future. But somehow, whenever I woke up the next day I always had a feeling that this couldn't be what life was all about. That this wasn't the purpose. That there should be more. Much, much more. No, people are not meant to be on this earth just to fight an addiction.

It was only when I truly understood why I gambled, and when I could replace my addictive thoughts and behavior with positive and constructive ones that disrupted the addictive pattern that real and lasting changes occurred. Now, I haven't gambled in over four years. My life has gone from debt, loneliness, and a messy apartment with closed curtains, to a rich and fulfilled life. I've used the strategy that I used to break my addiction to break other bad habits (which means either stopping it altogether or simply refraining from overindulging), such as drinking too much on a Saturday night and watching over two hours a day of television.

Now I want to share the strategy that worked successfully for me, with the rest of the world.

I've written this workbook, first and foremost, for you, the struggling addict. I wrote it because I know from experience that it can destroy your life. I wrote it because I can't stand to see so many wonderful souls being torn down by the devilish claws of addiction. I wrote it because I know there is a way out. Even for the worst struggling addict.

Just quitting your addiction is one thing. It is what you get back when you quit or no longer overindulge in something that you feel true joy. Besides the incredible change in my financial situation, health, productivity, and social life, the change I am most excited about is the change in my consciousness. Finally, I feel strong, secure, and self-confident enough to experience life fully. I'm no longer in my head all the time, which allows me to finally connect with the people I love so much, as well as new people. I can enjoy the fruits of life with integrity, as I can respond to any personal problems in a strong and constructive manner. This feeling of control, of enjoying life and most importantly, of truly connecting with other people, is worth every struggle that the gambling addiction brought to my life.

This workbook is not only intended to help you with quitting your addiction. It is also intended to help you to start over. To create and *live* the life you deserve. Because, after all, don't you at least deserve to experience a bit more joy than the chains of addiction?

How to Read This Workbook

With this step-by-step workbook, I want to inspire and help you to take back control over your own life by not letting addiction be the guiding force of your life anymore. This book shares the same 7 simple steps I went through to quit my destructive habit: gambling addiction. I made it a structured and practical workbook that is intended to help you instantly or at the very least inspire you to take the steps necessary for you. The book guides you into a better understanding of your addiction. The reason *why* addiction is present in *your* life. Most importantly, this workbook will give you tools to solve problems your addiction has caused and to be proactive in creating a meaningful, joyful life. A life where you will be strong and secure enough to deal with the inevitable problems of life. And where you will deal with these problems consciously, without hiding in the horrific claws of addiction.

The time indicated under the steps is, of course, a mere indication. It could help to follow this timetable, in order to make your addiction process more attainable. If for whatever reason you won't go cold turkey or your goal is only to stop overindulging in your addictive behavior, I absolutely welcome you aboard. I want to inspire you to take back control of your life. For almost all addicts that eventually means quitting altogether. But it's up to you. Take your time if you need it.

As we all know, recovery doesn't simply require the fulfillment of some steps.

Especially when accounting for the processes of revealing what kind of feelings you are trying to hide by turning to your addiction, recovery is a procedure that could take months. And for some much, much longer. But even in a shorter period of time, you can take giant steps to proactively deal with the consequences of your addiction, building up the inner strength to combat your addictive cravings. And most importantly you can find meaning in your life by working on your talents, connecting with others, and enjoying life to the fullest.

I would recommend to immediately start with the guided 90-Day Journal on page 79. This daily writing prompts will surely help to improve the recovery process, better understand your addiction, and strengthen the relationship with yourself. I would recommend to reflect on one question each day and read and use the workbook simultaneously.

Note to the Reader

As stated in the disclaimer, this book is not intended to act as a substitute for medical advice or treatment. Any person with a condition requiring medical attention should consult a qualified medical practitioner or suitable therapist. Addiction can sometimes become physical, especially when you have severe alcohol or drug addiction. Also when suffering from severe mental problems, it is wise to contact a suitable therapist. Listen to yourself and to your body, and never be too proud to ask for help.

A book is merely a book. Words are merely words. In and of themselves, they bear no magic. But you, within yourself, have the power to transform words. Into hope. Into better thoughts. Into better actions. And eventually, into change.

Don't be discouraged when you don't see overnight results. Because that's not the purpose of this book. And, I guess, that's not the purpose of any recovery method. Addiction is a giant that can only be taken down by small steps. If the only thing you get out of this book is a clearer and stronger intent on why you want to quit your addiction and how you're going to do it, that's perfectly fine.

For some this book, these words will bring more. Discover what it brings to you. And remember, don't be too hard for yourself. Please don't. A little love for yourself can go a long way. It is the announcement of a new dawn. And I sincerely hope that this book will help you to find that new dawn. To eventually stop addiction. Put an end to it. Find recovery. And then, find a new life. Your life.

Step 1 - Quitting The Pattern

Day 1

The first step in your journey to a new life without addiction is a simple one. Just don't do it anymore. Don't smoke your cigarettes anymore, stop playing the roulette, stop overeating. Simple, right?

Simple, yes. Easy, no. Not at all.

Quitting your addiction might as well be one of the hardest things in the world. It means conquering an ingrained habit. It means changing something that you've been doing day in and day out, for a long period of time. It has become second nature. And whatever we say about addiction, it is something that has helped you enormously over the last few years. It has protected you when you needed it most. The addiction numbed your deep feelings of pain. But since you've purchased this workbook, you and I both know that those days are numbered. No longer is addiction the solution. The addiction is an even worse place, despite its distraction from your deepest pains. Today will be the first step on your journey to change. Wake up from this nightmare. Meet your new dan.

In step 1 of this workbook, we will go over these 4 points that will help quit your addictive pattern. These can very well be the start of your new, addiction-free life.

Quitting our addiction? Do it smart.
- **Share your story.**
- **Stop.**
- **Seek help.**
- **Cut off resources.**

Quitting your addiction? Do it smart.

This is really important. As stated in the disclaimer and in the note to the reader, this book is not intended to act as a substitute for medical advice or treatment. Take this statement to heart. Going cold turkey isn't always safe when your addiction has become physical, such as in cases of alcohol or drugs. Keep this in mind. I was a heavy gambler, a true addict. I've tried to control my gambling behavior before, but at a certain moment that simply wasn't helpful anymore. The only solution for me was to quit altogether. Find your way. Be honest with yourself. Quitting your addiction? Do it smart. And it's you who, deep inside, always knows best.

Share, stop, and seek help.

One of the biggest breakthroughs I had during my recovery process was sharing my story. It was just after I had made an attempt to quit gambling altogether. This unfortunately wasn't my last attempt, but the sharing of my story was crucial in eventually conquering my addiction for good. It was on a Wednesday night, just the day before I went through a long and devastating gambling period. I lost almost 2000 Euros, which was a lot of money for me at that time. When I woke up the following day, I decided - no more! That night I called one of my dear friends. After some preliminary chit chat, I was finally courageous enough to share the real reason for my phone call.

"I have a problem, and it's been going on for quite some time now. It's a gambling problem."

I was at my parents' house at the time. Nobody was home. I remember walking through the house while telling the story. My friend listened, as the very best of friends tend to do, and he offered help. It was after one more relapse that I decided to take his help. Yet sharing my addiction story was one of the best feelings I had during those dark years of gambling. It lifted the weight off my back and eventually reassured me that I didn't have to be on this journey all by myself.

That's why my advice is to share your story.

It will take courage, but it will be a huge step to freedom - to breaking down your addiction. If there is someone in your life that you can share it with, someone that won't judge you, then that just might be the person to which you can tell your story. But practice the conversation in your head. This will make it easier when you have to do it in real life. Additionally, discussing the issue over a phone call might be easier than doing it face to face. If you don't have a friend, family member, or someone else to call, share it somewhere else. There are online forums or Facebook groups for people with your addiction, where you can share your story either anonymously or not. Alternatively, you could share it with a professional, anonymously with a professional helpline (telephone or chat), or a support group.

This first step, like any other first step, could easily be the most difficult one. Sharing your dark, long-kept secret may be one of the most challenging hurdles you'll ever overcome. And it's worth the struggle. By sharing it, the heavy pressure of your addiction will feel lighter, and all of a sudden you're not alone in your fight anymore.

Stop.

If you want to quit your addiction, there is no other way than to first say: 'It's over now, I'll quit.' Even if your purpose is only to lessen your addictive behavior (for example by only gambling once per week with a specific budget, smoking three cigarettes a day, or drinking only two glasses of alcohol and only on the weekend), it's a great first step to stop altogether with your addictive behavior for a period of time. It's crucial to be one hundred percent behind your decision to quit. If you're a spiritual person, it will help to ask your God for help in this process. If you're not spiritual, ask your Higher Self to guide and guard you in the quitting process.

The conscious decision, and following through, of quitting your addiction, are steps that are attainable for all addicts (except when it's a physical addiction and you need medical assistance). I absolutely believe that every addict, whether suffering from an addiction to pornography or overeating, social media, or gaming, can stop his or her addiction for at least 24 hours. If you do it right, I am quite certain that you'll be able to add another 24 hours.

And another.

> **"When you make the conscious decision to quit your addiction, don't make it solely about the quitting itself; try to see what you could gain."**

Don't make it harder for yourself than it needs to be. Only the act of reaching that first milestone of 24 hours should give you a reason to celebrate. So celebrate if you've made it to the first 24 hours, celebrate again when you make it to 48 hours, and so on. Do this for at least one week. Find a healthy pleasure that isn't your addiction, like watching a movie with friends, taking a walk in nature, or buying yourself a little present. We'll discuss these options further in step 2.

I know the horrors of addiction. That's why the quitting process should be something wonderful. Of course, there are lots of responsibilities to attend to after you've quit, like financial consequences, health problems, needing another diet, and deteriorated relationships. And of course, we'll deal with these problems in step 3. But there's more. When you make a conscious decision to quit your addiction, don't make it solely about the quitting itself; try to see what you could gain. A life of freedom, however, you define that for yourself. Wearing that beautiful dress with confidence, being able to buy you friends dinner, being in a great condition, having a wonderful night out without being mean, because you're drunk or on drugs, and so on. That joyous and compelling dream or, when you haven't really defined your ideal life yet, at least the absence of addictive horrors will move you forward in the first days of quitting your addiction.

Seek help.

"Ask for help. Not because you are weak.
But because you want to remain strong."

Les Brown

When you've made the decision to quit, don't be alone. You could share your decision with the friend, family, professional worker or group you've contacted to talk about your addiction. Asking for help doesn't make you weak; it is the only smart way to know your weaknesses and give yourself the extra power of another person or support group to fight something as big as an addiction.

Define for yourself how you want to be helped. For example, the option of calling someone when you're having a really hard time with your addictive thoughts, having an accountability buddy, or simply ask the other person/support group what they suggest. For most addicts, it is one bridge too far to really seek professional help, and yes, there are other ways to do it. But it's going to be hard to do it all on your own. So at least share your story and find the courage to ask for help in whatever way suits you best. Like we went over in *Share your story*, you could also do it anonymously, online, or with a professional helpline.

Cut off resources.

What's critical in the quitting process is cutting off from resources that fuel your addiction. These could mean access to your money, to certain websites, to unhealthy food, alcohol, casinos, etc. By cutting yourself off from these resources, you will make it so much easier on yourself to actually follow through on your recovery. You could do this together with the person or group you've gone to for help.

When I made my final attempt to quit my gambling addiction, more than four years ago, I asked my good friend to take control of my bank account. He took over my banking passes and access to online banking. If you make it difficult for yourself to indulge in your addictive behavior again, you have a better chance of succeeding.

If you want to you can find a **healthy** substitute for these resources. I still had some money, but it was cash money that my friend gave me. Or instead of bottles of wine, have bottles of a healthy soda you absolutely like, and so on. Don't change a bad habit for another bad habit. But use your imagination and pick something from the thousands of positive, healthy options this universe has to offer.

A Last word of Encouragement + Empowering Exercise

It's very easy to start blaming yourself during this period. It can be devastating thinking about all the problems you've caused with your addiction... Stop for a moment and consider your achievement of this day.

The day you quit. The day you stood up to your addiction. The day you said no the destructive and the decline and yes to a richer, more authentic life. To a new beginning.

You need to be your own best friend in this period (and for the rest of your life). Pat yourself on the back for taking this enormous step to committing to quitting your addiction forever. It's probably the most courageous thing you've done in your life so far.

Statements Exercise

A good way to emphasize this is by putting empowering statements/affirmations on sticky notes around your home or on your smartphone. There are countless free affirmation apps for your smartphone that can help you with this! A good exercise, for now, is to come up with at least 5 to 10 empowering statements/affirmations that will guide you through the initial stages of your recovery.

So why not do it right now. Sit down and write statements that speak to *you*.

Hereby a couple of examples:

There is so much more to life than the pain and suffering from addiction.

Addiction is a waste of my time.

Life in recovery is absolutely authentic for me.

Addiction is a lie, my spirit is the truth of recovery.

Only a fool waits for addiction to make him/her happy

Addiction is killing my energy for life, recovery is my new energy.

The Universe/God is guiding me from the darkness of addiction into the light of recovery.

Recovery from the lies of addiction is my new way of life.

I am so much more than the destruction of addiction.

There are thousands of positive, creative options to spend your time on in life.

There are a lot of rules for affirmations, but just write down what **you feel is right**. Sometimes *negative* affirmations, such as 'Affirmation is killing my time', can be extremely helpful in the beginning stages of fighting addiction. Especially when you mix it with positive statements.

The next level is to record your statements on your smartphone and listen to your statements/affirmations over and over again. When you go to work, when you cook, before you go to sleep, when you sleep, and so on. Change your thoughts, and you diminish the power of addiction significantly. To make it even better, you can put on some music under your statements to emphasize these statements. Search for 'audio mix' in the play store or apple store to easily mix your statements with motivational music (instrumental music, such as movie soundtracks is highly recommended).

I added this exercise because, after the initial setup, it can be easily done without much effort. Just simply put in your earphones and go for a walk. Give your mind a different tape to listen to, then the destructive thought patterns of addiction. Listening to the statements can also bring up emotions, especially when you mix it with inspirational music (such as movie soundtracks). This can open up the possibility to release and confront the emotions around addiction. And find new fuel, more intention for change.

Of course, this *statement exercise* alone won't override your addictive thoughts. It's only a tool to help you during recovery. To emphasize where you don't want to go and where you *do* want to go. But you need more than affirmations to change. So we're going to find the patterns. To educate ourselves. To take responsibility. To find a new vision. And eventually, you will discover lasting recovery. So try out this exercise a couple of times for yourself, see how it works for you.

Because when it comes to recovery in general, there are no gurus. There are just teachers that can bring you to the truth within. Who can show you ways or methods to release thoughts, powers, that are holding back who you really are. The utmost reason why I would like you to try out this exercise is my belief that changing your thoughts almost always changes your reality. And, as all the exercises in this book have benefited me, this one especially has helped me enormously in my own recovery.

Summary - Step 1

- *Quitting your addiction? Do it smart.* Read the disclaimer of this book and the note to the reader.
- *Share your story.* Don't pull the full weight of your addiction all on your own. Find someone to share your story with.
- *Stop.* However you want to deal with your addiction, quitting it right away is the best way to conquer it. Stop and celebrate every day, for one week at least, that you've made this first step. Make it not only about quitting your addiction, but also about what you will gain when you quit.
- *Seek help.* In whatever way suits you best. It's really hard to quit totally on your own. *"Ask for help. Not because you are weak. But because you want to remain strong."*
- *Cutting off resources.* If you make it difficult for yourself to indulge in your addictive behavior again, you have a better chance of succeeding.
- *Statements/Affirmation exercise.* Changing your thoughts almost always changes your reality.

Step 2 - Replace Your Addiction & Find Peace

Week 1

When you've made the incredibly first step of quitting your addiction, you will be left with more freedom. But this freedom is not what we addicts are used to. The addiction was our strongest habit; without this, we feel naked. And also probably in pain and bored. It's crucial in the first days and weeks after you've quit your addiction, to replace your addiction with something else. That is what we are going to do in step 2 of this workbook. Also, we will take the first steps in unraveling your addiction.

- **Discover your pattern.**
- **Replace your addiction.**
- **Make sure to do it.**
- **Take notes.**

Discover your pattern.

A new life is awaiting you. How beautiful... Unfortunately, it's not only sunshine. There will be rain and storms. Apart from the costs of your addictive behavior, which we will cover in step 3, there is also an undeniable craving to go back to your old habits. These habits, however bad they were, were your ultimate comfort zone. Now, after a hard day of work, you won't allow yourself to drink a glass of wine, smoke a couple of cigarettes, eat a nice, big cheeseburger, or play World of Warcraft for three hours. No, you know for a fact that this addictive behavior is only making life worse. But instead of taking a glass of wine, what do you do now?

You have to understand that our addiction comes from craving.

I gambled whenever I was bored, irritated, depressed, or had financial problems. My own feelings and circumstances lead me to my addictive behavior. The first step in replacing your addiction is understanding when your addiction pattern. This is a very practical approach, which will help you prevent relapses down the road or deal with them in a strong and constructive manner whenever they do occur. So take note of the moments when you started engaging in addictive behavior. Think about circumstances, certain people, feelings, and thoughts. Write down as many details as you can think of. If you want, you could use the notes pages at the end of this workbook.

Next, look at all the moments you've written down and try to find a pattern. Are there certain feelings, thoughts, people, or circumstances that led you inevitably towards your addictive behavior? Write these patterns down. This will give you the golden information: *your addictive pattern*. Whenever this pattern occurs during the first weeks of your recovery process, remember that you can change the end result of the pattern. First, it was an addiction, but now you can replace it with something else (see the next point of this chapter). In step 5 of this workbook, we will also go over how to interrupt your addictive pattern during its initial stages.

In the first stages of conquering your addiction, you probably see your addiction as the enemy. It is important to get to know this enemy. Let the following quote guide you during these initial stages of your battle with addiction:

> *"If you know the enemy and know yourself,*
> *you need not fear the result of a hundred battles.*
> *If you know yourself but not the enemy,*
> *for every victory gained you will also suffer a defeat.*
> *If you know neither the enemy nor yourself,*
> *you will succumb in every battle."*
>
> Sun Tzu, *The Art of War*

Replace your addiction

When you know your pattern, you can change the outcome. You can also interrupt the pattern. Later in this workbook, we will go further into interrupting your pattern, but for now, it's good to simply know your pitfalls.

To replace the outcome of addiction, find one or two easy alternatives to your addiction that bring you release and healthy pleasure. Don't think too hard on this, it should be something you like very much. In my first three weeks after quitting my addiction, I started watching The Sopranos. Besides that, I did an evening walk every day to clear my mind. I recommend doing one truly pleasurable activity where you don't have to be super engaged, and one thing to clear your mind, such as walking, sports, singing, or meditation. Also, when you have a physical addiction, such as overeating, cigarettes, or alcohol, replace this habit immediately. So find a diet (which is probably the easiest thing to do nowadays, there are thousands of choices. Just choose one and commit to it. That, the commitment and rigid structure are the only reasons a diet works), an alcohol-free drink and something to replace your cigarette, a breathing exercise for example.

This is an interesting story about a fellow gambling addict who also replaced his addiction, right after he decided to quit. He told me that for the first week after he quit, he felt so tired that he decided to take a one hour nap each day, right after work. Two hours later he went to play tennis with his best friend, who knew his gambling secret. He told me that the very act of scheduling in his nap didn't make him feel guilty, because he knew he needed it. By scheduling it in for a specific time period, he was the master of this little habit of napping. That feeling of mastery, even if for a seemingly silly but necessary activity like taking a nap, was (so he told me a couple of months later) what gave him the confidence to believe that if he could master one action, he could master another. And another. And his addiction.

What is important to understand is that you are already working on being a master over your addiction. You are reading this workbook. You've done or will do the exercise of the earlier paragraph to understand your addictive pattern. So if you work on this process every day, even if it is only for ten minutes a day, you absolutely deserve time to enjoy your day or at least find a little peace. Addiction isn't over when you've made the decision to stop. To deal with all of this, it's important to give yourself some relaxation and peace to charge your battery. Make life meaningful even in difficult times.

Make sure to do it

When you've chosen one or two alternatives, make sure you do them every day for at least a week. To make sure you do them, plan them in at a convenient time. Schedule them into your agenda. These actions will be something to look forward to in these difficult days and it will be something you could hold onto. By actually planning them in, you will make it real for yourself. Now, it will be much easier to follow through and give yourself some needed distraction and peace.

Take notes

Take notes during your recovery process. Have one special notebook, or use this workbook as your personal notebook.

Write down your thoughts and feelings during your recovery process. Like a diary. This way you can discover your changes over time. By putting your thoughts and emotions on paper, they will get out of your system, at least for a moment. They go from the darkness of your pain to the light of your consciousness and there, and only there they become solvable. The process of writing will give you a lot of inside in your addictive processes, and in who you are as a person.

Remember Sun Tzu's quote,

> "If you know the enemy and know yourself,
> you need not fear the result of a hundred battles."

Summary - Step 2

- *Discover your pattern.* Write down your addiction pattern. Think about thoughts, feelings, and certain people. From these moments, find your pattern.
- *Replace your addiction.* Find one or two alternatives for your addiction and start implementing them into your life.
- *Make sure to do it.* Schedule these activities into your life, so you actually follow through on them.
- *Take notes.* Write down your thoughts and emotions during the recovery process. The process of writing will help you learn about addictive processes, and who you are as a result.
- **If you want dail recovery inspirations, follow me on Instagram: become_recovery**

Relapse

*"It's okay. Why do we fall Bruce?
So we could learn to pick ourselves up."*

Batman Begins

I sincerely hope you haven't, but if you've relapsed, pick yourself up. The road to lasting recovery is a hard one. There are many hurdles, mountains even to overcome. There are no spotlights for the recovering addict, no cheering stadiums, but it's nevertheless a road worth Olympic Gold. And thus, we'll fail from time to time. It doesn't have to be a relapse, it could be something different. Learn from it and march on.

Don't be too hard on yourself.

The incredible pain you feel whenever you relapse, is because you feel that there is never going to be a solution to the problem. That you will be left behind in the darkness. Try for a moment to distance yourself from this moment. See yourself three, five, or ten years later. Having a nice dinner with family and friends. It's one of these dinners. And for a moment you remember your successes of recent years. That moment, that dinner is way closer than you might think. It is already here when you decide to pick yourself up again. And again.

Step 3 - Take Responsibility & Educate Yourself On Your Addiction

Week 2

After you've completed steps 1 and 2, there is a little distance between you and your addiction. You're not chained as a slave anymore. Your hands and thoughts have freedom. That being said, in no way will this release you from your responsibilities. Most probably because of your addiction, your problems have piled up. Think about financial consequences, health problems, and deteriorated relationships.

It's time to meet these responsibilities and take care of them.

This means taking responsibility for *your* addiction. Besides the problems, you're facing, also educate yourself on what addiction actually is, so you will be stronger when your addictive cravings surface again. This way, you will preserve yourself and won't burden others anymore by the consequences of your addictive behavior.

In step 3 of this workbook we will go over the following points:

- **Create an inventory of your problems and make a to-do-list**
- **Educate yourself**

Create the inventory of your problems and make a to-do-list.

When you feel strong enough, it is time to take responsibility for the problems that you've caused with your addiction. It's best to first take care of yourself. Like in any emergency, make sure you yourself are safe. Then it's time to deal with the consequences. I strongly advise you not to wait too long with this. It hurts to confront yourself with the consequences of your addiction, with all the pain you have caused yourself and others, but don't walk away from this suffering.

I am moved and inspired by Viktor Frankl, a psychiatrist who survived Auschwitz in World War II. He wrote a well-known book entitled *Man's Search For Meaning* about his experiences at the concentration camp, which he survived. I want to share an excerpt from his book here:

"The way in which a man accepts his fate and all the suffering it entails, the way in which he takes up his cross, gives him ample opportunity—even under the most difficult circumstances—to add a deeper meaning to his life."

The lesson herein lies, that we as addicts, who've suffered tremendously during our addictive periods, even though we mainly brought it upon ourselves, could make this suffering meaningful when we deal courageously with the consequences. This means, dealing as responsible adults with the consequences of your addiction and finding out why you're addicted, and learning from these sufferings in the past to create a meaningful present and an inspiring future.

Here are the three steps that can help you to solve your problems over time, and more importantly to take ownership of the consequences you've caused because of your addiction. You could start immediately with these steps after you've decided to quit your addiction, and sometimes you absolutely have to because external factors require you to do so. If it is not so urgent, and you want to come to your senses first, you can wait a couple of days, or maybe a bit longer, to do so. But don't neglect them. There are a lot of lessons to be learned from cleaning up the mess. It can be refreshing to take responsibility. Like spring.

The first step is to make an inventory of the problems you've caused by your addictive behavior. Write down a list of all the consequences you're now faced with. Think of financial problems, deteriorated relationships, inner conflicts, a messy house, health problems, not taking care of your appearance, etc.

The second step is to create one or more solutions for each of these problems. To make it practical, break these solutions down into at least one action item you could do immediately to help solve each particular problem. For example, when you are in financial debt, your ultimate solution could be, *make an extra 500 USD on the side each month*. An immediate solution could then be, *call or email all my creditors and make* *appointments about realistic installments to pay back my loans.* Or when you are enormously overweight, your ultimate solution could be, losing 50 pounds in 6 months. An immediate solution could then be, *Start exercising 30 minutes a day and choosing a diet.*

The third and final step is to take action. Break down the solutions of step 2 into actions and create a to-do-list. Then, schedule these actions. What will help is to do one action immediately, so you give yourself a reference point that could help combat the consequences of your addiction, however large they are. Like in the example given above, you could make the immediate calls and emails to your creditors, going for a 30-minutes, interval run and buying the food necessary for your diet. What can help is to write down your *why* for this to-do-list. Remind yourself *why* you're doing all this. Help yourself with writing down and/or listening to your own empowering statements every day. To see, feel, breathe the reasons behind your actions. Then calling a creditor, becomes something different. It becomes part of a mission. The embodiment of a new beginning.

Educate yourself.

Taking responsibility for your addiction means also making the chance of relapsing as small as possible. Make your ability to deal with addictive cravings as strong as possible. You could do this by educating yourself on addiction. You've taken the first step in doing so already, by defining your addictive pattern in step 2. In this workbook, we will focus heavily on your inner thoughts, feelings, and conditioning regarding your problems, deepest pain, and addiction. This is inevitable when you want to tackle the roots of your addiction and bring about lasting change. To make this journey easier, it is important to know at least some basic knowledge about addiction. Know the problem you want to solve.

The way to do this is to educate yourself about addiction in general and your own addiction in particular. For example, I read many forums about gambling addiction, read a scientific book about gambling addictions, some other books about addiction in general, and watched Youtube videos about the topic. This really helped me in understanding addiction, but more importantly in understanding my *own* addiction. Every addict is unique, but by taking in information about addiction, you will better understand your own.

There is an extensive list of good resources on addiction online and I've added some at the end of this book.

During the actions of step 3 of this workbook, keep taking notes. During this stage of your recovery process, because you are taking responsibility for your addiction, taking action in solving your problems, and educating yourself on addiction, you will have a lot of new insights. These will be worthwhile to write down, as they can help you tremendously in your recovery process. Knowledge is (potential) power.

Summary - Step 3

- *Create an inventory of your problems and make a to-do-list. The first step* is to make an inventory of the problems you've caused by your addictive behavior.

The second step is to think of one or more solutions for each of these problems. To make it practical, break these solutions down into at least one action item you could do immediately. *The final step* is to take immediate action.

- *Educate yourself.* Taking responsibility for your addiction means also making the chance of relapse as small as possible, and the ability to deal with addictive cravings as strong as possible. You could do this by educating yourself on addiction, so you know what you're fighting against. An extensive list of resources for educating oneself is at the end of this book.

Step 4 - Create 1 New Habit

Week 3

When I look back at my recovery process, what helped me to put a big distance between me and my addiction was creating a new habit. When I was in my third week of recovery, I decided to take on one new habit. At that time, I already had some knowledge about the importance of habits. I had read *The Power of Habit* by Charles Duhigg and I had watched several Youtube videos of people who decided to take on a new habit. They all shared stories about how this one new, positive, and constructive habit had changed their lives. The quote of Aristotle echoed in my mind:

> *"We are what we repeatedly do.*
> *Excellence, then, is not an act but a habit."*

- **Choose a habit.**
- **Choose a duration.**

Choose a habit.

The habit I choose? Simple as it sounds, a morning ritual. Now about one year later, I realized the enormous impact of having a constructive habit. That's why I absolutely believe that adopting such a positive and strong habit early on in your recovery process could be a gamechanger. Because it is something you hold on to, no matter what happens. Something that is quite easy to do, something positive, and something that you could do at the same time day in and day out.

Among the things I do during my morning ritual, is to take a shower, drink lemon or ginger water, write down three things I am grateful for, and three things that excite me in life, write down my goals and affirmations, and watch an inspirational video on Youtube. I've done for almost one year now and it has transformed my life, yet again. Every day I start my day with awareness, a sense of direction, gratitude, and passion.

That's why I highly recommend you do the same. Choose a habit that is quite easy to do daily and that will help you - over time - to create more awareness in your life. For this will help you to enjoy life more intensely. And to deal with life's problems more strongly, more calmly and with less anxiety and stress. Remember, take it one step at a time. My recommendation is to first establish one habit, and if you want to transform your life even further, pick up another one. If you've established your first habit, then and only then go for another habit.

Examples of new habits you could create
- Morning ritual
- Meditation
- Writing in a diary
- Visualizing of your goals

- Reading inspirational books for 10 to 20 minutes a day

More specific habits could be related to your specific addiction,
- Drinking 5 glasses of water every day
- Eating at least 2 pieces of fruit every day
- Save at least 1 USD every day in a savings account that you don't have access to
- Go for a walk for at least 15 minutes every day
- Doing 10 pushups a day and one extra every other day

Choose a duration.

There are several opinions on how much time you need to establish a new habit. You hear 21, 30, 40, and 66 days most often. I chose to do my morning ritual for 66 days, to ensure I established the habit. After 66 days of doing my habit, I started a new habit for 66 days: reading inspirational books for at least 20 minutes a day. After you have chosen your habit, choose a time frame, and start immediately to integrate this habit into your daily life. Again, don't overdo it and start with just one habit at a time.

Summary - Step 4

- **Choose a habit.** Choose a habit that is quite easy to do daily and that will help you over time create more consciousness in your life so that you can enjoy life more fully and with the ability to deal with life's

problems with self-confidence and security. Examples: meditation, morning rituals, keeping a diary.
- **Choose a duration.** After you have chosen your habit, choose a time frame to integrate your habit, and start immediately. Do one habit at a time.

> *"We are what we repeatedly do.*
> *Excellence, then, is not an act but a habit."*
>
> Aristotle

Step 5 - Meet Your Addiction and Rewrite the Script

Week 4

In step 5 of this workbook, we will explore the following questions more deeply: why are you addicted? And how can you actually halt your addictive pattern? The first part of step 5 is about meeting your addiction and taking a deep look at yourself *and* at the problems that lay behind your addiction. The second part is a more practical one: how to interrupt and rewrite your addiction pattern.

I'll advise to first read this whole chapter before practicing because rather than proceed in chronological order, the points in this chapter are meant to be integrated together.

- **Meeting your addiction.**
- **Creating a new pattern.**
- **The alarm bell.**
- **Rewriting your script.**

Meet your addiction.

"Don't let the addiction and all attached problems sit in the shadows, it's there in the dark, where evil breeds. "

If you want to quit your addiction, you should understand what it is. I had multiple relapses before I finally successfully quit. I believe that the main reason for my successful recovery is that I could deal with life's problems in a manner different than just falling back on my addiction. Also, I now had a big enough purpose to quit, because of my new goals and principles that replaced my old unreliable ones. We will go on to rewriting your script later on in this chapter. For now, it's time to meet your addiction. I will start with an example of my own meeting, to make it clear what I mean when I say 'meet your addiction'.

It has always fascinated me, the amount of control one has over themselves when you take charge. This means that you could ask different parts of yourself about certain behaviors, feelings, and thoughts, and get an answer. You could do this by talking out loud to yourself in a quiet place, or out in nature, or asking questions in your mind while sitting in silence. If you're not familiar with self-talk, journaling is a great start.

Opening up to yourself could be a long process, where a lot of patience is required. However, I've noticed both by myself and with other addicts that the initial stages of this search for answers could occur quickly. For example, the first time that I asked the following question – *"Why do you want to gamble in excess?"* – I received a shocking answer: *"To destroy you."*

When I asked the following up questions, I came to understand that my addiction:
- Wanted to protect me from inner pain
- Was a cry for something more exciting in my life (variety)
- Was a desperate way to solve my financial problems.

These answers helped me enormously in tackling the core of my addictive problems.

**"The more you practice self-talk,
the better and more insightful answers you'll get."**

So this is the first step, to get to the core of your addiction and define your real problems. Seek within yourself the real reasons for your addiction. You could try different ways of finding these answers, as described earlier. Talking out loud, journaling, or in silence. It's about opening up to yourself. Don't let the addiction and all attached problems sit in the shadows, it's there in the dark where evil breeds. Bring it to the light of your awareness because there - and only there - healing, responsibility, and a new life begins.

A good first question to start this process is:
"Why do you...?" or *"Why am I...?"*

(Fill in the blank with your addiction. For example, drinking in excess, smoking, doing drugs, overeating, playing video games multiple hours a day, etc.)

For me, it worked best to direct my answer to the addictive part within myself. So I asked, the "Why do you...?" question. You could also direct the answer differently, and start with "Why am I...?" It's up to you. To have the most success with this process, it's important that you start in a quiet state and then begin to question yourself. A short meditation, peaceful music, or a quiet walk before you start the process, can therefore help. If you don't succeed the first time, don't worry. Try it another time. The more you practice this self-talk, the better and more insightful the answers will be.

After your first question, you can get the conversation going. Asking multiple 'why' questions could help you to come to the core of your problems. Taking notes during this process is recommended.

A last note: be your own best friend in this process, as talked about in step 1 of this workbook. Compliment yourself for this enormous step. For dragging the addiction out of the darknesses. For bringing it in the light of your awareness. You're taking back control over your life and taking responsibility for your problems.

Creating a new pattern.

"When you repeat this process of dealing with your problems consciously, this will become your new pattern."

When you start doing this soul searching, you'll find the reasons for your addiction and define the problem. The addiction served a purpose, like everything else we do in life. Addiction gives you immediate pleasure, or at least a time out from real life's problems. To exactly define those problems is a crucial step in a lasting recovery. Already in the first step in this workbook, you defined the pattern of your addiction. That, together with the first point of this chapter, will provide you with important insights about your addiction. With this knowledge, you can start interrupting your old addictive pattern. Knowledge is power, but only when you use it right.

You need to take ownership of your addiction, which means dealing with its underlying problems. Back to my own example. These were the underlying reasons for my addiction:

- Protection from inner pain
- A cry for something more exciting in my life (variety)
- A desperate way to solve my financial problems

I did some deep soul searching to discover the reasons for my inner pain and found the answers. On a more practical level, I solved the latter two reasons for my addiction. I began to do more exciting things in my life - I joined a theatre group, started singing lessons, wrote my first book, and started my dating life. As for my financial problems, I made appointments with my creditors about paying back my loans, started to save a little bit of money each month, and budgeted all the money that came in.

So, for some of your reasons for addiction, you just need practical solutions. This means interrupting your addictive pattern. We as addicts are really good at hiding in our lonely rooms. Isolation: curtains closed, door locked. Most of the addiction occurs when we're alone, in the 'safety' of our own rooms. So, if you're familiar with this pattern, you should interrupt it. Easy as that. Open the curtains, open a window, call a friend, chat on Facebook, go out for groceries, and so on. Literally, let in light, break the loneliness, it's the ultimate place for addiction to grow. Whatever your pattern is, you should find a way to interrupt it. This way, the wire of your addictive pattern is broken and your addiction is slowly worn down.

The root cause of most addiction is deep inner pain. Examples are missing love, missing connections with other people, or feeling insignificant. To solve these root causes will take a lot of time. It could be worthwhile to talk about this pain with a dear friend, a family member, or even talk about it with a therapist of some kind. If you feel uncomfortable doing that, you could also work with yourself, through deep inner conversations. For myself, it has helped to talk with a therapist about my problems, but for the most part, I've dealt with my deep inner pain by doing extensive self-talks. When practicing this more and more, I felt a deeper connection with myself and I felt the presence of a Higher Help that truly guided me to find the answers I so desperately needed.

While this is a long road, the root causes of your addictions won't have to bring you any longer to addictive behavior at the beginning of your recovery process. Not having the deep feeling of loneliness anymore, which is something else entirely than being lonely, won't go away within a couple of days of self-talk or talking with a therapist. Though, you could deal with this feeling differently, right away.

Instead of hiding in the darkness of your addiction whenever you feel lonely, interrupt this pattern.

Talk with yourself, or journal about why you feel lonely. If you don't feel strong enough at that particular time when you feel the pain, doing another activity will stop the pattern. Among good alternative activities are, calling a friend, sports, singing, taking a walk, buying groceries, watching a motivational Youtube video or just distract yourself for an hour or so with some innocent pleasure, like watching comedy. Make a deal with yourself that you will deal with your feeling of loneliness another time and actually schedule this time into your agenda.

The crucial difference is, that instead of numbing yourself from the pain, you decide to consciously deal with your problems. Addiction no longer is an option. When you repeat this process of dealing with your problems consciously this will become your new pattern. Yes, a new habit.

The alarm bell.

"The addiction is you. You are not your addiction, but addiction is a part of who you are."

The next paragraph is one of the most important concepts of this book. We all know that your addictive feelings of course won't go away forever when you decide to quit for good. Instead of fighting against it, use your addictive feelings as an alarm bell. Because they do serve a purpose, namely: there is something wrong. When you start recognizing this, your addictive cravings could serve you enormously. Instead of giving in to the craving, you could simply ask the question, 'What is there I need to hide from in my life right now?' And deal with the answer in a different way, not with the destructive solutions of your addiction.

The use of this *alarm bell* has helped me greatly over the last few years.

So far in this workbook, I've talked about the addiction as the enemy. In the first few weeks of your recovery process, this is very helpful, because there are so many negative feelings about your addiction, that seeing it as the enemy does not only feel truthful but also will help you to stay sober. Who wants their enemy to win, right? Eventually, you have to acknowledge that the addiction is not your enemy.

The addiction is you. You are not your addiction, but addiction is a part of who you are.

By accepting this and even embracing this, a whole new set of possibilities will open up for you. Everything you accept as a part of you is something that you can control. It is not anymore alien, a force outside your control. No, it is inside of you and you are the king of your own kingdom.

Personally, I have accepted the addiction as a part of who I am. I talk to this part of myself every now and then and make sure that it won't sit on the throne of my kingdom again. But it can be, like any other part of my personality, a great advisor. Now, I see my addiction as a friend. Because of the loud voice of addiction, I always know exactly when something is wrong in my life. I thank my addiction for speaking up and then I decide to solve the problem in a constructive manner.

Rewriting your script.

"We will act consistently with our view of who we truly are, whether that view is accurate or not."

Tony Robbins

So, what have we covered so far? That you can get to the core of your addiction and define the real problems. When you've done this, you can interrupt the pattern and create a new one. Instead of dealing with your problems in a destructive way, you take back control of your own life and deal with them in a constructive way. In the final part of this chapter, we'll make sure that there are no loose ends in your recovery process anymore. What I mean by that, is that you rewrite the image of yourself as an addict.

These are examples of defining yourself as an addict,
- I'll always drink too much
- I can't stand the craving for overeating
- I am a smoker

> **"When you have the script of an addict, it's going to be almost impossible to find lasting recovery."**

With these principles, it's going to be really hard to quit your addiction for good. There is this well-known story of a man who tries to find his way in Chicago, he has a map but got lost all the time. The reason? He has a map of Boston. When you have a map of an addict, it's going to be almost impossible to find lasting recovery. What you need is a different map. The first exercise in this book, about writing and listening to the statements is a good first step. But that's it. A first step. To really live from a different map, you need to go deeper within.

So bring your old addictive script into the light. Write down all your thoughts, that label yourself as an addict. Thoughts could be,

- I'll always fall back into my addiction
- I am not strong enough to stop
- I can't resist the temptation

Take a look at these thoughts, is this the script that will help you to become the hero in your own movie? No, it's merely the script for the first part of your movie. The part where the hero lives his second choice life. Now the time has come, when you say: *'I can't take this anymore, I want a different life!' So, you need a different script.*

It's time to write down new principles that will help you to come to a different life; to be the hero in your own movie.

These should be principles that resonate with you as a person. Some empowering examples for your recovery process could be,

- When a problem arises in my life, I deal with it consciously and constructively
- I am a master of my addictive cravings, and only use them to know that there is something wrong in my life, but I'll never give in to them.
- I will dedicate my life to sharing with others, developing my talents, and giving love, I'll see my life as too valuable to indulge in destructive habits such as ... (fill in the blank with your particular addiction).

In the next coming days make a definite set of principles, that will be your script in your new life. Then, for at least one week (I recommend doing this for 21 days), write down and/or say out loud these principles every morning and every night. Don't just write or say them out loud, but really feel these words. Feel the meaning and potential of these affirmations, how they are going to change your life for the better. Furthermore, hang down these set of principles in your room and/or as a note in your smartphone (or download an affirmation app and customize it into your own principles), so you could see and reflect on them daily. Over time, these set of principles will become your new script, and you will act consistently with how you define yourself, right now. A new hero, a new you, is born.

Summary - Step 5

- *Meet your addiction.* If you want to quit your addiction, you should understand what it is. With self-talk or journaling, get to the core of your addiction and define the real problems.
- *Creating a new pattern.* Interrupt your old addictive pattern, by taking ownership of the underlying problems. Deal with these problems consciously and over time this way of dealing with problems and pain will become your new pattern.
- *The alarm bell.* Use your addictive feelings as an alarm bell. Your addictive feelings come up, whenever there is something wrong in your life. Thank your addiction for speaking up. Then decide to solve the problem in a constructive manner. To not give in to your addictive cravings.
- *Rewriting your script.* When you have a script of an addict, it's going to be almost impossible to find lasting recovery. First, become conscious of your old addiction script. Second, create a new script that will truly help you in your recovery process. Lastly, intergrain these principles into your mind, by writing them down and/or speaking them out loud and reflecting on them daily.

What to do when you relapse?

This is a short intermezzo: what to do when you relapse. Recovery, like everything else in life, is a bumpy road. And yes, of course, it can happen that a relapse occurs. It's not the end of the world.

A relapse is *not* the end of the world.

It is your reaction to the relapse that makes the difference. So go ahead and think about it for a moment. Not with fear. Or a *knowing* that addiction sooner or later will return anyway. Because there is definitely a chance that addiction for you never again will return. But if it does, it's better to know how to greet the little beast.

So, go ahead and write down three to seven steps on what you're going to do or can do when relapse occurs. How can you interrupt the pattern of your addiction so to speak. Can you call someone? Is it possible to take a time-out? Is it possible to limit the damage? Or, what can you do after your addictive binge? Be creative.

And by doing this exercise you can see how much bigger you are right now than your *addicted self*. See now how much you've already grown. For a person who can be aware of his lower self, is not too much separated from being in control of that lower self.

Yes, that can be a good thing about this exercise. It can give you even more control. Inspires more love, more care, more self-responsibility, and self-confidence within you to even deal with the worst of the worst of situations. And by knowing that you can, the chance of those situations ever happening again will decrease drastically.

Step 6 - Create a New Vision and Take Action Today

Week 5

*"If you don't know where you are going,
you'll end up someplace else."*

Yogi Berra, *Famous Baseball Player*

The first 5 steps of this workbook are mainly directed to take control of your addiction. Now it's time to take back control over your life. In order to do that, you need to know what you want. By creating a compelling vision for your life and by taking immediate action (small steps), you will start to feel the magnitude of your own capabilities and the limitless possibilities of life. The change you've always been looking for is not years, months, or weeks away in the future. That surprising possibility for change is right now.

- **Create a vision.**
- **Create goals.**
- **Take action today.**
-

Create a vision.

"How many of these potentially life-changing decisions are waiting to be made?"

A while ago you made the decision to quit your addiction. In order to successfully continue on your way to lasting recovery, it's crucial to not let it be just about addiction. What I want to share in this workbook is that life after addiction is possible. It's time to create that life.

Everything in life has two creations.

We are all familiar with the second creation - the buildings around you, great sporting victories, an outstanding movie. But before this actual creation, there is the first creation. An idea, a thought, an instinct, that is made into a plan and set into motion. Sometimes it doesn't take more than a couple of seconds. You see an incredibly attractive person, you'll notice a tingling feeling and maybe approach this person. Within those milliseconds, between feeling and walking up to this attractive stranger and actually starting to talk, there is a decision. That decision has the potential to change your life.

If you look at your own life, how many of these potentially life-changing decisions are waiting to be made?

I bet there are many. And I bet that you have a hundred excuses why you haven't or won't make them. In the first part of this chapter, it's time for you to put your ideal life on paper.

Without any hesitation, without any fear, create the life you really want to live. We only have a brief time on this earth – why would we stay in the prison of our own fears and negative thoughts, or the prison of the supposed judgment of others? While fluctuation in life is normal, you don't want to catch yourself in a downward spiral for decades, years, or even months. Take matters into your own hands and determine your course.

> *"Know, that one day this life could be yours,*
> *and the start of all of this is happening right now."*

So, take your notebook and create a compelling vision that is truly yours. Make it a vision for three, five, or ten years down the road. When you've finished it, write down the purpose behind your vision. WHY do you want to be in a relationship? WHY do you want to become a millionaire? WHY do you want to build your own company? This purpose is the driving force behind your ideal vision. When you have a vision and know for yourself why you want to achieve it, it will be easier to take the action necessary to achieve it. This purpose makes it not just a vision of the mind, but also of the heart.

If you find it easier, you could first gain an overview of your life by making a Life Box. Think about all the important areas of your life and put them in a different box. The different areas could be Family, Career, Health & Fitness, Friendships, Religion, Self-Growth, Contribution, Relationship / Dating Life, Finances, Traveling, or Hobbies. You will most likely have somewhere between seven to eleven different boxes. The next step is prioritizing these different areas and ranking them in order of importance. With this information, it could be easier to create a vision where you'll include all the things you so desperately want.

Lastly, we don't all have to be new J.K. Rowlings, Steve Jobs, or Leonardo DiCaprios. Simply write down your vision. It doesn't have to be *big* in order to feel right. Just make sure that it isn't a vision created from fear, but that it is a vision from deep within yourself. A vision of truth. A vision that reflects what you want, that reflects your purpose on this planet. When you're finished, visualize this vision for a moment. Put on some good music and see yourself living the life you've just put on paper. And know that one day this life could be yours, and the start of all of this is happening right now.

Create goals.

"A vision without a plan is almost impossible to achieve."

Your vision is a great beginning to change your life, but it's not enough. A vision without a plan is almost impossible to achieve. What we're going to do is break down this vision into achievable goals for the foreseeable future. This could be one month, three months, or up to a year away. With these short-term goals, there will be an undeniable call to action and you will begin to start walking the steps to your compelling vision.

I will use my own example of how you could break down your compelling vision. Among other things, I had a vision of being a best selling author, having a loving relationship, and being financially independent. For those larger, ultimate goals I made the following shorter-term goals:

One year
- Written a sci-fi novel
- Dated at least one woman who I have a genuine connection with
- Save 1250 Euros and earn an extra 150 Euros per month by either extra work or a raise in salary

Three months
- Write the first draft of the first part of my novel
- Date a woman
- Save 250 Euro and either receive a raise in salary or start working on the side

One month
- Write out the outlines for my novel and finish the first chapter by writing at least 30 minutes every day.
- Approach at least one woman every time I go out, start using a dating app
- Budget my money properly, read one book about how to handle your finances, and save at least 10 Euros.

All of these short-term goals helped me to come closer to my ideal vision. Not only that, I already felt like I was living my ideal life. I wasn't a best selling author, but I was writing. I wasn't in a loving relationship, but I expressed myself and made honest connections with women. And no, in no way was

I financially independent, but finally, my savings account was bigger than zero. The lesson is to first create attainable goals, so you can get started and create momentum.

Take action.

Your goals are your plan to achieve your ideal vision. But a plan without taking action is useless. Or like the famous quote says, *The distance between your dreams and reality is called action.* The small steps you will take today lead you one step closer to your ideal vision in life. These actions will make you feel like you're already living that life. Start today. It could be something simple, like making a financial budget, coming up with five potential titles for your new blog, reading five pages of an inspirational book, or having a nice dinner with your family. As long as it is a step in alignment with your ideal vision and your goals in the foreseeable future.

One more thing.

Your ideal vision and your goals are not written in stone. They can fluctuate and they should be organic, like all things in life. Things can occur that will impact your vision and goals. We can't control everything that's going on in our lives. It's paradoxical. You need to be very persistent and consistent when you want to achieve your goals in life, yet you also need to allow flexibility so that you can alter your life goals when circumstances change or your ever-changing interests demand a new course and new goals.

You can always decide what *you* want in life.

Don't let your dreams and desires be beaten down by everyday life and worrisome thoughts. Whenever a situation calls for a radical change in your life plans, rely on the purpose and values behind your ideal vision. They can guide you once more to a new path in life.

Summary - Step 6

- *Create a vision.* Create a compelling vision that is *truly* yours, without fear and hesitation. Make it a vision for three, five, or ten years down the road. When you've finished this, write down the purpose behind your vision.
- *Create goals.* A vision without a plan is almost impossible to achieve. Break down your vision into achievable goals for the foreseeable future.
- *Take action today.* A plan without taking action is useless. Start today. It could be something simple, as long as it is something in alignment with your ideal vision and your goals in the foreseeable future.

Step 7 - Stay Inspired

The Rest of Your Life

" Reinforce positive, constructive and inspiring thoughts in your mind every day."

During your recovery process and indeed, during the rest of your life, there will be moments of discouragement. Times when everything you've set out to do seems impossible. Setbacks that make you hear your addiction screaming at you from the caves of your being. Slowly but surely, your new set of principles, your understanding of your addiction and its pattern, your vision, and your goals are giving you a new foundation that will handle these problems. That will handle the fearful and negative thoughts. A foundation that is without inner sickness, that is both solid and flexible. That can handle both rain and sunshine, tears, and laughter.

What will help you in this process is always staying inspired.

What I mean by this is that you reinforce positive, constructive, and inspiring thoughts in your mind every day. You can do this by reading inspirational books, watching motivational videos on Youtube, joining a support group, or talking to a coach from time to time. Or simply by keeping a healthy, strong relationship with yourself. Through honest self-reflection. And to increase your awareness about yourself and life. By doing this on a regular basis, you take on a whole new set of empowering beliefs in your subconscious, so that eventually, making constructive choices will feel like second nature.

At the end of this book, there is an extensive list of inspirational books and Youtube videos that can help you stay inspired.

The Nature Of Addiction

A Final Chapter

The nature of addiction is very closely related to contraction. Because attention, in periods of addiction is totally contracted. It is limited to the craving, to the activity you are craving for. Drinking, gambling, sex, eating, and so on. The easiest way out of any addiction period is to broaden your attention. To look around you, to be aware of the infinite nature of reality. It is not necessary to put your awareness that huge, just realizing there is more than your craving, more than the particular addiction activity will be sufficient to get you out of your gaze, your binge momentarily. Realize very well that nothing really chains you to your addiction.

Whatever anyone tells you, shifting your attention during moments of craving or an addiction binge is perfectly possible.

In fact you may have had these moments yourself. The key is to extend these moments, to embrace them and to fall in the greater awareness instead of locking your attention to craving. In the moment itself, the moment of pure craving it is very hard to shift your attention for a prolonged period of time.

So the key is to practice this shifting of attention in times when that craving is not too much present.

When there is a beginning urge try if you could shift your attention to something else: the landscape you are in at that time, listening to an audiobook, or an uplifting song, greeting a stranger on the street, having a glass of water, lying on bed for a while, go for a run, drink a cup of tea, and so on. The possibilities are endless. Just that realization will empower you: the possibilities are indeed endless. It is a hard lie of your addict personality that all your attention should be directed at your craving. That there is nothing else more important than the next drink, than getting money for your gambling habit. Because simply it is not true. The conversation, the talk of your addict personality is full of lies. They're the limited truths in the contracted reality of addiction. But that contracted reality is only a tiny small part of life. It is like you are staring at the ground the whole day while walking through the beautiful city of Paris. You miss the nice streets, the beautiful trees, the loving couples, the art, the dynamic of the city. Because all you are looking at are the stones on the street. You will see dirt, shit of pigeons and cigarette butts. And although you may have invested all your time and energy that day on looking down at the street, that is not reality as a whole. Far from it. Simply looking up once would've given you a whole different outlook in life.

The key to overcoming addiction is to shift your attention. To expand your awareness. Make a list of other things beside your craving you would like to put your attention in. How about your loved one's, or self-care, or watching that tv-show, or creating a painting, or starting investing in crypto, or going for a walk, or making a smoothie, or taking a bath, or calling an old friend, and so on. Make a long list of all the things you rather put your attention on than your craving. That action alone would expand your awareness big time.

Determine how you can make your life more exciting.

Because as with all things, your addict personality doesn't only tell lies. There is truth behind the craving as well. And often it has to do that you are strongly unhappy about parts of your life. One of them, almost always, is that you miss true excitement. Not the seeking for intensity, but the authentic excitement. The soul-like, inner-child rush to create, to dance, to connect, to live. So put your attention on all the things you would love to experience, even if they at this moment may seem very far away from you. It doesn't matter.

When you put attention to these exciting experiences, bringing them in your field of attention, the chance of it showing up eventually will increase. Because the physical manifestation is the final step, the steps before that happen in your imagination. So bring it there, write down the things you truly want to experience. Write down that trip to Hawaii you would love to make, the soul mate you would love to meet, the passive income you would love to earn, the charity you would love to support, the photo art you would love to make, the tennis lessons you would love to start, the new appearance you would love to try.

Bring attention to other things than your craving.

Stop running around in that small circle of craving. It has been known now: the craving for drinking, the drunken binge, and then the hangovers. That tiresome circle has been repeated over and over and over and over and over again. So bring some new, energy filling 'circles' into your life. Bring your creative force to life. Because you are a creator. Maybe not an artist that births paintings or a novel, but you are a creator of new energy, new goals, new experiences, new feelings, new thoughts, new beliefs. So use it. It is your inherent quality.

That special creator quality is what all humans possess: so yes, by all means start using it. Don't waste that talent: bring it to practice. And it doesn't have to be big to begin with, you don't need to build your own house immediately, or earn five thousand dollars passive income immediately, or find your soul mate immediately: start small. Start with finding pictures of houses you are fascinated by, start writing down what you would do with five thousand passive income per month, connect with the people that are already in your life. By doing these small acts you start creating the feelings that are present in your bigger vision.

And so you are starting to walk towards a life you love.

Recovery of addiction doesn't happen overnight, but starting to shift your attention can happen indeed today. The process of shifting attention can be a lot of fun. So embrace it, embrace your talents, embrace the creator within you, embrace all the other positive, exciting, authentic, joyful things you can put your attention on. And slowly but surely start moving away from contraction, by opening yourself up to the infinite possibilities that are surrounding you.

If you like content similar than this: check out my metaphysical book on addiction recovery: *Shifting Attention: The Curious Tale Of Addiction & The Magical Art Of Recovery*

The book is available on Amazon as ebook, paperback & hardover.

The End.

It's up to you now.

First of all, I want to thank you for purchasing my book and congratulating you on coming to the end of this workbook. Although I don't know you, the simple fact that you've made it to the end tells that you have the absolute spirit to quit your addiction and change your life for the better. I am certain that the steps in this workbook will guide you, combined with your own techniques, your own spirit, and mind, towards lasting recovery. Towards more happiness. Towards the shining light of your true purpose in life.

Final Thoughts

There will be days when all that we covered, all the work you've put in and all your good intentions may seem useless. Times when it will be difficult to sit down and do what you know you have to do.
To put on your running shoes or to say the kind words you want to say to your loved ones. Hours where you want to close the curtains and lock the door. Minutes where you feel down, fearfully, and stressed. Moments where the will to act

courageously, to act from the heart, is threatened by devilish temptations. You are going to make mistakes and different problems will arise. There will be fresh tears and unhappy moments.

Lasting recovery won't change that.

But it will give a new perspective and hope in the beginning, and it will give purpose and energy later on. Then you will feel the strength, deep within you, to deal with the storms and rain as *you*: a strong, resilient and caring person. You will feel peace of mind, courage, and an undeniable feeling of self-confidence and a love for life.

And there will come a moment when you fully enjoy the fruits of your work and the safety of your outstanding character, a moment where you dance, have one of these rare, great conversations, or walk on a magnificent island with your loved one... There, glancing over the blue water and feeling a tingling breeze on a sunny afternoon, you will stop for a moment. Realizing, without a single doubt, that all of the struggle, all of the pain and all of the tears have been worth it.

C.W. Van Straaten

PS. Don't forget to check out the following pages. The 90-Day Journal starts on page 79. I wish you all the best!

Inspiration & Education

Books

Overcoming and Understanding Addiction

Recovery: Freedom from Our Addictions by Russell Brand
Healing the Addicted Brain: The Revolutionary, Science-Based Alcoholism and Addiction Recovery Program by Harold Urschel
The Biology of Desire: why addiction is not a disease by Marc Lewis
The Disease to Please by Harriet B. Braiker
No More Mr. Nice Guy Robert A. Glover
The Power of Habit by Charles Duhigg
Portrait of an Addict as a Young Man: A Memoir by Bill Clegg
The Presence Process by Michael Brown

Self-Growth (General)

Levels of Energy by Frederick Dodson
The Big Leap by Gay Hendricks
The Six Pillars of Self-Esteem by Nathaniel Branden
The Subtle Art of I Don't Give A Fuck by Mark Manson
The Slide Edge by Jeff Olson
Think and Grow Rich by Napoleon Hills
Outwitting the Devil by Napoleon Hills
Unleash the Power Within by Anthony Robbins

Feel The Fear And Do It Anyway by Susan Jeffers
Tools of Titans, by Tim Ferris
The Art of War by Sunzi
The 5 Second Rule by Mel Robbins
The 7 Habits of Highly Successful People by Stephen R. Covey
No Excuses! The Power of Self-Discipline by Brian Tracy
The 12 Week Year by Brian P. Morgan
The War of Art by Steven Pressfield
The Self-Exploration Journal: One Year. A New Question Every Day by Zen Mirrors

Inspiring and Spiritual

The Way of the Peaceful Warrior by Dan Millman
The Alchemist by Paulo Coelho
The Power of Now by Eckhart Tolle
Man's Search For Meaning by Viktor Frankl
Ego is the Enemy by Ryan Holiday
Levels of Energy by Frederick Dodson
Intimacy by Osho
Courage by Osho
The Little Prince by Antoine de Saint-Exupéry
The Prophet by Kahlil Gibran
The Portrait of Dorian Gray by Oscar Wilde

Finance

The Richest Man in Babylon by George Samuel Clason
Secrets of the Millionaire Mind by Harv Eker
Unshakeable: Your Financial Freedom Playbook by Anthony Robbins
Money Master The Game by Anthony Robbins
The Cashflow Quadrant by Robert Kiyosaki
Rich Dad Poor Dad by Robert Kiyosaki

Youtube

https://www.youtube.com/watch?v=dOkNkcZ_THA 5 Lessons To Live By - Dr. Wayne Dyer
https://www.youtube.com/watch?v=PIFEPX0C_s&list=LL20t-pbWR9vlHDK89Cc5X3w&index=15 Powerful Meditation
https://www.youtube.com/watch?v=LMmuChXra_M Ohm meditation for Sleep
https://www.youtube.com/watch?v=dizQH0lxH6k Ohm Meditation
https://www.youtube.com/watch?v=F5pKqKwEs-s&list=LL20t-pbWR9vlHDK89Cc5X3w&index=17 Motivational Video 1
https://www.youtube.com/watch?v=XfIWymEfwFc&list=LL20t-pbWR9vlHDK89Cc5X3w&index=7 Motivational Video 2
https://www.youtube.com/watch?v=vf2We-AEtmc&list=LL20t-pbWR9vlHDK89Cc5X3w&index=13 Motivational Video 3
https://www.youtube.com/watch?v=k-T0v8nNKE0&list=LL20t-pbWR9vlHDK89Cc5X3w&index=10 Motivational Video 4
https://www.youtube.com/watch?v=j8rYt2WhJoU Motivational Video 5

The 90-Day Recovery Journal

Nothing is more helpful than honest self-inquiry when you try to change your behavior. This 90-Day journal will deepen your understanding of addiction, life's purpose, and your strengths and weaknesses. And it will increase your awareness about yourself and about life. It's therefore the ideal tool to strengthen your recovery process and the relationship with yourself. Each day the journal offers you a new thought-provoking question or short empowering exercise.

Both the questions and exercises are placed in a specific order to create lasting benefits. When using this journal for just five to twenty minutes a day, you will see tremendous changes in your life. Immediate changes in how you feel, insights about your past, and long-term changes regarding self-acceptance and self-confidence.

The benefits of this journal
- Learn how to turn obstacles into opportunities
- Look at your addiction in an astounding different way
- Feel a sense of calmness, while new and inspiring thoughts are created Create immediate changes in your finances, health, and relationships
- Go to the roots of your Inner Pain and start the healing process

The questions in this 90-Day journal are coming from my newly released *The Addiction Recovery Journal, 366 Days of Transformation, Writing & Reflection*. With this one year guided

journal, you can take your recovery process and personal growth to the next level. If you want to purchase this journal, this is the link to it:
www.amazon.com/gp/product/1720269351/

I sincerely hope that journaling will be just as an effective, soothing habit for you as it is for me.

Day 1

If your addiction was a person, how would you describe him or her? What is the one piece of advice you would give him or her?

Day 2

What could other people learn from you?

Day 3

What does recovery mean to you?

Day 4

What would happen if, for the next thirty days, you said no when you wanted to say no and yes when you wanted to say yes?

Day 5

30 Day Challenge. Pick a new small, constructive, and simple habit and try it for the next 30 days. Examples: Reading for 10 minutes a day; drinking a smoothie a day; making your bed every day, or meditating for five minutes a day.

Day 6

If you would take ten percent more responsibility for your own happiness, what would happen?

Day 7

What would be a better way to deal with your hurt feelings?

Day 8

What triggers your addiction? Name up to three triggers.
What are other ways to deal with these triggers

"The enemy is a very good teacher."
The Dalai Lama

Day 9

If your addiction was the enemy, what could you learn from it?

Day 10

Write down three things you can do
to deal better with setbacks in life.

*"Insanity is doing the same thing over and over again
and expecting a different result."*
Albert Einstein

Day 11

Name three small actions you can take to calm your mind.
Do at least one of these actions today.

Day 12

If you had the strong belief that your decisions are under your control, how would life be different for the next seven days?

Day 13

Write down three intelligent things you can do to prevent a relapse.

Day 14

Write down at least seven reasons
why your addictive behavior is irrational.

Day 15

Describe the purely evil side of your addiction. Name at least one thing/thought/person/dream that could serve as a light against the darkness of your addiction.

Day 16

Name ten things you're grateful for in life.

"At one point, we all consciously decided how much to eat and what to focus on when we got to the office, how often to have a drink or when to go for a jog. Then we stopped making a choice, and the behavior became automatic. It's a natural consequence of our neurology. And by understanding how it happens, you can rebuild those patterns in whichever way you choose."
Charles Duhigg, *The Power of Habit*

Day 17

When did your destructive habit start?

_____

_____

_____

_____

_____

_____

_____

_____

Day 18

Write down three good things you can do to deal with boredom?

_____

_____

_____

_____

_____

_____

_____

_____

_____

Day 19

What role does procrastination play in leading up to your addictive behavior? What is one thing you could do to battle procrastination?

Day 20

What would your life look like in three months if you stay on this recovery journey? And in a year?

Day 21

What is the root cause of your addiction?

Day 22

Write down an empowering response to the addiction thought, *recovery is boring.*

Day 23

Has addiction been a means for you to flee from reality?
If so, what is it that scares you so much?

Day 24

What gives you hope?

Day 25

What would you want people to understand about your addiction?

Day 26

Are you afraid to let people see your true colors? Why or why not?

> *"The price of inaction is far greater than the cost of making a mistake."*
> — Meister Eckhart

Day 27

What dreams have you delayed because of your addiction?

Day 28

Name 12 things you're grateful for in your life.

Day 29

If you allow yourself to make mistakes, what would you do differently tomorrow? And what would you have done differently in the past?

Day 30

What are your three best character traits?

Month 1

A Morning Ritual

During my recovery journey, I've learned many new things but none of them had such a profound impact on my life as creating a morning ritual. It is transforming to start the day by taking control of your morning. No Facebook feeds or news claiming your attention, rather you will take the time to prepare yourself for the day. This habit alone, could be a game changer during your recovery. On Day 33 there is an exercise for creating a morning ritual. For now, here are five examples of what I do when I wake up (in chronological order):

- Write in my dream journal
- Take a shower
- Drink hot water with ginger
- Do five minutes of exercises, such as push-ups
- Write down my intention for the day: 1 or 2 major goals, and 1 or 2 minor goals

Day 31

Sometimes during an addiction binge you might have (had) the feeling of "losing it all". Somehow that doesn't always feel so frightening. In fact, it could be the thing you look forward to... Losing it all. Or, did you actually long for a new beginning?

Day 32

What does happiness mean to you?

Day 33

What would be a constructive and positive morning ritual for you?
Try it for three days.

Day 34

How often did you tell yourself, "I am worthless,"?
Is it time for another statement?

Day 35

Is there a dark side lurking beneath your surface?
If so, how do you treat it?

Day 36

Would it be an idea to meet with your dark side kindly
and let it express itself in a healthy way?

Day 37

What is the pattern that leads to your addiction?

Day 38

Write down one or two things you can do to interrupt the pattern that leads to addictive behavior.

Day 39

Write down the key lesson you learned from your addiction.

Day 40

What advice would you ten-year older self give to you now?

Day 41

Addiction has an enormous power. If that power and energy is yours, and you could use it for something constructive, it could make a huge difference in your life. For what area / specific action could you use ten percent more energy?

Day 42

What is your purpose in life?

Day 43

What about last week makes you feel grateful.

Day 44

Who would you like to be one year from now?

Day 45

Describe a past experience where you overcame failure.

Day 46

What did you learn from overcoming failure in the past?

Day 47

What can you do on a daily basis that is easy, fun, and positive?

Day 48

If you no longer searched for recognition, how would life be different?

"When I let go of what I am, I become what I might be."
Lao Tzu

Day 49

What did you tell yourself to become an addict?

Day 50

If you could be ten percent more positive,
how would tomorrow be different?

Day 51

Write down three things you can do to be more kind to yourself.

Day 52

Write down at least five positive experiences/insights during your recovery journey.

> *"Start small and keep it simple. That's our motto for change."*
> 21 Exercises, *The Secrets For Self-Growth*

Day 53

Is a childhood wound still running your life today?
What could be the next step towards accepting and fixing it?

Day 54

What is a small step you can take right now
that will lead to a better life?

Day 55

How would your seven-year-old-self describe you?

Day 56

What is keeping you in the past?

Day 57

Are expectations holding you back
from experiencing the here and now?

Day 58

What would you like to do tomorrow?

Day 59

Write down a list of all your skills and qualities.

Day 60

How has struggling with addiction shaped you positively?

Month 2

Taking Small Steps

A lot of people who are into self-development and yes, recovery is a part of that, are falling into the trap of wanting too much in a short amount of time. This willingness is where get-rich-quick gurus build a fortune off. However, *lasting* change doesn't happen overnight. It's an in-depth self-discovery journey combined with taking consistent small steps that will lead to the big changes. It *will* take time, however. And that's okay. The journey itself is where you could focus and where, between hard lessons and thoughtful moments, you will find joy and confidence about your silent progression.

Day 61

What advice would you give someone else in recovery?

Day 62

What is something in the past you feared but did anyway?

Day 63

What does being lonely mean to you?

Day 64

What do you look forward to in the near future?

Day 65

When was the last time you had to *pick yourself up*?
How did you do it?

Day 66

Release your worries and negative thoughts on paper.

*"God, grant me the serenity to accept the things I cannot change,
the courage to change the things I can,
and the wisdom to know the difference."*
Serenity Prayer

Day 67

What is something you have to accept?

Day 68

How did addiction trick you?

Day 69

Write down seven reasons why you believe you can recover from addiction for good..

Day 70

Write down three recent achievements that make you proud.

Day 71

What are you constantly searching for?

Day 72

What does your *Inner Voice* is trying to tell you?

Day 73

Are you validating yourself based on material things?

Day 74
What makes you a beautiful person?

Day 75
Is life trying to teach you a particular lesson? What is it?

Day 76

If a relapse happens, see it as part of the path to recovery. Write down five self-care activities you can do after a relapse.

Day 77

Are you ignoring your true calling?

Day 78

When was the last time you laughed so hard it hurt?

Day 79

Celebrate life. Treat yourself today or tomorrow with something that feels right and joyous. Write down exactly what you're going to do.

Day 80

What do you feel guilty about?
What first step could you take to forgive yourself / make it right?

Day 81

Are you still maintaining a secret life?

Day 82

How would tomorrow be different if you'd express yourself freely?

Day 83

If a writer decided to write a book about your life, what would be the genre? Comedy, drama, inspirational, etc. Why?

Day 84

When was the last time you gave someone a compliment?
Give a compliment each day, for the next week.

Day 85

Write down a list of compliments you've received in your life.

*"To be happy we need something to solve.
Happiness is therefore a form of action"*
Mark Manson, *The Subtle Art of Not Giving a F*ck*

Day 86

Problems are an inevitable part of life.
What problems would you like to solve?

Day 87

What is your body trying to tell you?

Day 88
What makes you feel embarrassed?

Day 89
What is the life you deserve to live?

"Be yourself; everyone else is already taken."
Oscar Wilde

Day 90

What kind of self-talk helps you improve?

Month 3

Don't Be Too Hard On Yourself

Regret is a logical consequence of making the *wrong* decisions in the past. Certainly when these decisions became a pattern and created destruction. Yes, addiction inevitably leads to regret. But not just regret; anger closely follows. Maybe you initially felt anger towards certain circumstances, people, or even God, or the Universe. However, there is no escape. At some point, you have to look in the mirror and take responsibility.

When you confront yourself with your past mistakes it's easy to fall into self-blame. I believe in letting out the emotions (in a civilized way). From there, try to make things better. First of all, understand and accept that a recovery journey is tough enough already. You don't need another enemy. You need a friend. So at the very least, be your own friend. Help yourself. And recognize the fact that deciding you want to quit your addiction and taking the small steps to do so is already an enormous accomplishment.

About The Author

C.W.V. Straaten is the author of *The Addiction Recovery Workbook, The Addiction Recovery Journal, Win The Morning Win The Day, The Gambling Addiction Recovery Journal* and *The Gambling Addiction Workbook*. After living in several countries, the author is now traveling the world, working on his inspiring self-help guides and a children's book.

You can reach Mr. Van Straaten by email at cw.vanstraaten@yahoo.com. He doesn't do consulting, but he does read all his mail.

If you want Daily Recovery Inspirations follow me on Instagram. I have created this page to help you focus on becoming free from addiction & focus on recovery every day.

Instagram: become_recovery

Or you can search on C.W. V. Straaten

The Addiction Recovery Workbook

Made in United States
Troutdale, OR
10/11/2023

13614567R00086